Not Every Woman Swooned

new poems by

Elaine Heveron

Plain View Press
P.O. 42255
Austin, TX 78704

plainviewpress.net
sb@plainviewpress.net
512-441-2452

Copyright © 2010 Elaine Marie Heveron. All rights reserved under International and Pan-American Copyright Conventions. No part of this book may be reproduced or distributed in any form or by any means, or stored in a data base or retrieval system, without written permission from the author. All rights, including electronic, are reserved by the author and her publisher.

ISBN: 978-1-935514-61-9
Library of Congress Number: 2010922422

Cover art by Deborah South McEvoy,
      "So Many Roles I Have to Play"; acrylic on paper
Cover design by Susan Bright.

*For Lou
my husband,
the man I love*

Acknowledgements

Thanks to the following publications which previosly printed the following poems: "Constant Fire," "My Burning Question" and (Zen Center) "Sangha" in *Illumination, Fire, Light and Heat*, © 2008, River Light Press; "If This Were The Last Day" and (Zen Center) "Sangha" in *Zen Bow*, 2009 and 2008, respectively; "The Trouble with Winter" in *Sifting Through the Words*, by Elaine Heveron, 2005; "White Sky" in *The Sky Above Us, The Air We Breathe*, © 2007, River Light Press;.

Thank you to everyone who has ever been a part of my life, even for a moment. Often I recall the things I have learned from each person I've known. Perhaps you shared a story, played some music, made a comment, or showed me some kindness that has had a profound effect on me. These gifts that relationships provide help to ease the losses and transitions we all have to bear in life.

Thank you to everyone who has ever bought or read my previous books, especially those who took the time to call or write to tell me that my work mattered to you. This book exists because of your kindness and caring ways.

Thanks for love and support— to Lou, my siblings — John & Patti, Pete & Suzie, Mary & Steve, Bernie & Liz, Amy & Scott, Marti & Chip, Mom, my nieces and nephews, my minions of cousins, the Faber family, the Manions, Mackenzies and Oshins, Mickie Neeck, Tracy Nowak, Cynthia Seefeld, Nancy Murrey, el jennings, Sandy Karlan, Ann Hood, Priscilla, Shae, Muriel, Robert, Dick, Rachel, Beth, Linda, Kathy, John, Colin, Bernie S. for the hand-made book bag. Mega thanks to Eric Heveron-Smith for sound editing CD version.

Thanks to Lisa Starr, Block Island writers, and BIPP teachers with whom I have been privileged to study.

Thanks to John White, for the chance to host Open Mic Poetry Nights at Equal Grounds Coffee House. Thanks to Steve O'Brien—for the intro on the spoken version, and for always encouraging me to write.

Thank you to Susan Bright for believing in me and giving me a chance to be published by "a real book publisher."

Contents: Not Every Woman Swooned

Acknowledgements   4

Summer

All You Have Is the Present	11
Moutin Reunion	12
Aural Love	13
It Hurts My Eyes To See	14
Sunflower Dreams	15
Brick Streets In the South Wedge	16
Weeds and Words	17
A Rolling Jar Of Honey	18
Letter to My Soul	20
Ontario Beach Park	21
Lost Journal	22
Lost and Found	23
Sewing Together, Worlds Apart	24
Shot	25
Taking My Back Yard Back	26
I Set Down	27
A Little Blessing	28
A Great Deal	29
Triggered Memory	30
Sangha	31

Fall

Now Your Words	35
A Rolling Bottle Of Wine	36
Leila In My Arms—	37
Mystie	38
Painted Lady	39
My Burning Question	40

Be True To Your School	41
Missing Dad	42
Statue Of My Father	43
Julia's Odyssey	44
Marti's Poem	45
Why Is It	46
How Was New York?	47
White Sky	48
Constant Fire	49
I Fall In Love Too Easily	50
Ginkgo Tree	51
Cleaning My Room	52
Your Untitled Artwork	53
So Far Away	54

Winter

In the Kitchen	57
After Valentine's Day	58
Landsdale Street	59
My Sister's Closet	60
Drano	62
Plain View Press Writer's Party	64
The Man For Whom I Used To Long	65
Odessa	66
Monterey	67
Isobel Illusion	68
Coffee Shop Scene	69
Boarding the Plane	70
January-March	72
Empty Oil Tank	73
I Feel You Kicking	74
Don't Say It (Insomniac)	75
Hoselton Toyota Waiting Room	76
Not Cleaning My Room	77

That Song	78
AWP — NYC 2008	79
A Former Beau	80
The Trouble With Winter	81

Spring

New Life Gossip	85
Billy and Me	86
The Trouble With Reading Your Poems	87
Memorial Day Rain Rant	88
Barely Spring	90
Not Every Woman Swooned	91
Breaking Twenties	92
National Women's Hall Of Fame	93
Peace Crane	94
Father Gregg	95
After Block Island Poetry Project	96
New Neighbor In the City	97
Early Spring	98
Highland Park In May	99
In Memory Of Doug Fetter	100
Confiserie Délices	102
If This Were the Last Day	103
About the Author	105
Alphabetical Index Of Poems	107

Summer

All You Have Is the Present

All you have is the present moment—
to breathe and be brave,
to love others—
and welcome love,
To accept your handicaps—
as you reach for the stars;
to grieve your losses—
and share your gifts;
to teach and to learn,
to reveal the hopes
in your heart, to sing
the songs of your soul,
to grow and transform,
from who you are now to
whom you are meant to be.

It's nearly impossible to live
each moment as if it might be
your last. Still — you can be
present to this moment, to
this pain, to this loss, to
this grief, to this love.
You can breathe.
And you can
be brave.

Moutin Reunion

Laser eyes
beneath intrusive
locks of hair
Two hands
commanding
drum sticks
Two arms
caressing
neck of bass
Piano creeps
in unafraid
to carry
the scene
Jarrett-like —
the keyboard
could be longer
and deeper,
causing
no trouble
at all — Sax
blows kisses
like a favorite
cousin on his
way to the beach
and somehow
   you
got to go along.

Aural Love

for Lou

Sometimes it's not
what you say — it
is only your voice
that I hear.
And it is not
my weak hearing or
poor listening skills.
It's just that the sound
of your voice is enough.
Yes—of course—
I am writing this
about you!
I'm a visual learner,
but an aural lover.
I adore the sound of
your voice. I shiver
in the hills and valleys
of your tonal range.
Your words thrill
like fireflies in the
celestial regions
of my brain.
Then, gone!
I cannot capture
or hold them—
nor would I.
Keep
speaking;
I'm closing
my eyes.

It Hurts My Eyes To See

for Lehna

Pouring lemonade from a teapot
   at La Tea Da, Lehna says:
*It hurts my eyes to see that
school bus across the street!*
(It's summer and she's nine.)
I say: *That's a great line—
can I steal it from you?*
   She laughs as we
both write it down.

She says she writes songs,
but they're not real songs—
Imagining the sweet songs
   in her mind, I think — Oh,
but what does real mean?
She knows what she likes —
   tigers, lions, elephants,
art and rhyme at the end
of her lines. She pulls her long
hair up into a pony-tail, eats
only the chocolate-dipped
   end of her strawberry,
sweetly asks the waitress
   for more chips, then
turns down dessert
   saying she is full.

But I can't get enough
   of this girl.

Sunflower Dreams

In my dream I have sunflowers
to plant in the corporate garden.
But I am told
there isn't any room.

In my dream
all the furniture
is being moved
into the future.
They are going
to steam clean
all the stains
of the past.
In my dream
I find a stash of small stuffed toys
in the corner of my boss's office.
I think: I'll have to talk to him
about giving these away
to needy children.

But in my dream
these toys speak to me—
They tell me they represent
his grandchildren,
his children, his youth—
and they belong here.

I wake up and find
a space for my sunflowers.

Brick Streets In the South Wedge

Even before I could see out the window
        of my father's car, I knew we were
getting close to my grandmother's house
        when I felt the textured bumpiness
of brick streets, after the long smooth ride
up St. Paul Boulevard and South Avenue.

Dad would let my brothers and me get
out of the car at her house and go ahead
to her door, pretending we had walked
all the way from Irondequoit. She always
indulged our joke, laughed when Dad arrived.
There was a hand-crank grinder on the wall
and her kitchen smelled of fresh ground coffee.
An oil cloth tablecloth covered the small kitchen table.
In the back yard, there was a perfect-for-climbing cherry tree.

On the way to Equal Grounds Coffee House this morning,
   we notice the brick base underneath the asphalt
being replaced on Caroline Street. Now we are
living only blocks away from where Grandma,
Dad, and his brothers lived on Nicholson
   Street from the twenties to the forties.

I close my eyes recalling the ride from
   Irondequoit to the South Wedge
   in my father's car and imagine my
grandmother — a few breaths away.

Weeds and Words

Why can't I pull words and lines
   from the air as easily as
unearthing weeds from
   the wet wormy ground?
Each one pops up,
like the arm of a child whose
teacher has called her name—
its pig-tail-like root shattering
clumps of dirt, and it's over.
One more intruder
to the zen garden left
to die in a bucket of twigs,
leaves and weeds. Who
planted their weird seeds?
Days and weeks of rain
have helped them grow,
enabled their easy removal—
Rrrrrip — and I win, every time—
in this solitary game. Who was
it who wrote on Facebook today:
I still like to play in the dirt. Well—
that got me going, this earth-mother
morn, standing in a full forward bend,
   hair in my eyes, pulling one creeper
at a time, enmeshed in the earthy task
of weeding, while dreaming of words,
and envisioning the layering of lines.

A Rolling Jar Of Honey

Whenever he ventured out
to the Highland Park
Diner, the Country Club
Diner or Jay's for breakfast,
Robert carried (concealed),
a small jar of clover honey.

One morning at Jay's Diner,
Robert added his usual
two teaspoons of honey
to a cup of black coffee.
Quietly placing the
honey jar under the
table, he began to flirt
with a regular waitress,
whose smile made him
shift his feet, knocking
the honey jar on its side.

Slightly cracked,
it rolled sweetly,
like sticky graffiti,
under his table, under
the next table, under
the next table, then under
the next and last tables.

Robert, who would never
put anyone out, was mortified,
his sweet secret revealed. Honey,
so tasty in coffee or tea,
now just a gooey mess.

Robert, always impeccably
dressed, forever heaping
praise on others, got down
on his knees, I'm sure,
so no one else would be
stuck with the chore
of removing that honey
from a linoleum floor.

No one remembers
if Robert ever finished
his coffee that morning.
I wonder if half of his English
Muffin remained — lightly toasted
and buttered — untouched, on his
plate as he completed a viscous
chore, washed his hands,
headed for the door.

Some say he never returned
to Jay's. That I don't know.
But I heard, after that,
he always drank
his coffee black.

Letter to My Soul

You are my Zendo
        and Buddha Hall
You are my confirmation name
You are my Godmother's strength
You are unconditional love
You are the raspberry
        bush in my youth
You are my cottage by the lake
You are my ardra chandrasana
You are my prana and mantra
You are my walk in the woods
You are a jazz singer at sunset
You are my laughter at bedtime
You are my internal rhyme
You are my father's warm smile
You are a worn piece of beach glass,
        shiny, and warm from the Sun.

Ontario Beach Park

The beach opens for swimming today:
       It is pouring rain—
as if the sun has never graced the sky,
       as if it never will.

Did you ever, as a kid, go swimming
unaware of the weather report—
       get caught in a downpour—
       snagged like a flounder
in a grand sweep of fishing net?

And did you imagine yourself:
       bearded, standing tall
in a fisherman's small boat,
       wearing a long white garment,
arms out, confronting the raging sea?

Then, as you lower your palms,
the waters ceasing their motion,
       would you glance at the sky—
see the clouds receed,
       surrendering to the light?

The beach opens for swimming today—
       I wonder—
Is anyone out there?

Lost Journal

Phil is right:
Stop looking.
      Let it go.
Assume it's gone.
      Forget about it.
There was nothing in there
      that I could not re-write
with my hands tied behind my back:
I could recite each page from memory.
      None of this is true.
I can't recall a word, except, oh, yeah—
      something like:

Why didn't I think to pray to
Poseidon when I was pulled
      down by the current?
I was five years old.

What comes next? Does it matter?
I didn't drown. My guardian angel
must have been promoted that day,
      since I went home breathing.
Maybe she wanted to teach me not to push
my luck — to manifest what would happen
if I kept on walking, further and further out —
      Lake Ontario was up to my neck.
All it would take is one underwater
      pothole and whoosh—
I was a child, unable to speak,
      begging for breath.

Lost and Found

Why didn't I think to pray
to the Sea God, Poseidon,
　when I lost my footing
in Lake Ontario? Did I pray
　to anyone—to Jesus?
　To God the Father?
　Mary or Joseph?
The Holy Ghost,
or, my favorite—St. Anthony—
the patron saint of loss?
I was lost underwater.
What about St. Jude—
the patron saint of lost causes?

I remember greenish water,
seaweed covered rocks,
the water's temperature
being the same as that of the air.
Real or imagined,
I recall spinning—
Was I, one of seven kids,
the sacrifice to Minotaur?
The was no silk string—
no white sail or flag to wave.
Perhaps the spinning,
I am realizing just now,
was the twirl of my body
as I caught your arm
and rose to the surface.

Sewing Together, Worlds Apart

for a woman in Jordan, who works at a sewing machine

Like a bird upgrading her nest with sticks
   and twigs, I find myself in the Fall
going through clothes, searching
   for weakening seams to repair.

This camisole I bought on sale at Macy's
is loosely made — only one zigzag stitch
holds the front to its back, holds an inch
of lace intact. It is marked *medium*, but is
way too large. So I sew — take it in, to make it
fit snugly, to hold in my warmth, come the night.

My portable cast iron sewing machine—
built when I was young — mimics the
clatter and hum of my mother's machine
in the fifties and sixties, and I feel a thread
of connection with the woman in Jordan,
who sat in the heat, sewing this for me.

As you ran this garment through the machine
   at which you sat, as you held it down flat,
could you imagine an American woman
   tailoring the piece you made like this?
From across the earth, I blow you a kiss.

Shot

Shot—
the hammock
snapped—
dropped
us down.
Shot—
the tulip heads—
stems left aground.
Shot—
the weeping
cherry.
Blink and we
miss its glory;
blossoms dust the
mid-May lawns.
Shot—
another
Rochester teen—
no words
to explain
or gang
to blame.
Shot — his
parents' dream
to smithereens.
Shot—
a prayer to
Heaven to
heal their
grief.

Taking My Back Yard Back

This is the year I am taking my
yard back from the squirrels—
going to homestead the lawn
furniture before they start
their diabolical cracking
of walnut casings, leaving
them in smithereens. I've
never tasted one of those
English Walnuts — never
got to bag them up with red
ribbons to give as Christmas
presents to family and friends—
I never get to see the outer green
hull ripen and shrivel off. They maw
the walnut casings into gross confetti,
scatter it all over the lawn and furniture
as they stand — *stand* — on my chair backs
and seats, holding and rolling, one at a time,
the wealth of walnut meat, as they watch me
watching them from my kitchen window seat.
   But not this year. This year, I'll wake up
     early, make coffee and toast, haul a
tablecloth and tray outside, as I wait
for The New York Times. I'll try and
ignore them, act as if I own the yard.
They'll stand on their little hind legs,
off to the side. Then, I'll look them
straight in the eyes and say, *nuts to
you, little buddies; this table is taken.*

I Set Down

I set down my empty glass of water.
I set down my hat and garden gloves.
I set down my bucket of weeds.
I set down my shopping and to-do lists.
I set down my agenda and calendar.
I set down my journal and pen.
I set down my need for appreciation.
I set down my expectations of others.
I set down my wish for a younger body.
I set down my list of complaints.
I set down my feeling like an outsider.
I set down my regrets on the journey.
I set down my fears of the future.
I set down my need to be every-
       where for everyone.
I rest my feet on a footstool—
       sit still, and sit still—
Today, I sit blissfully still.

A Little Blessing

We were in our hammock Sunday
   when it burst — to its demise
We didn't — 'til the next day
   see the blessing in disguise.
Before he joined me to lie back,
   I asked him, several times—
Do you think it is strong enough?
   I'm sure, he said, *it's fine.*
He was facing to the left,
   I was to the right. Together
we lowered our heads down,
   swung our legs up the other side.
We had only a moment of rest
   before the hammock swayed
and snapped. On the ground
   we lay there, facing skyward,
on our backs. He spoke to me
   and I glanced his way — *Are you
okay?* we asked each other.
   Don't know, we had to say.
Stunned from earth's hard slap,
   we stood up, without a sound,
stumbled past the hammock,
   laying loosely on the ground.
I noticed the thick metal frame—
   one of us could have fallen alone.
That hammock was ready to break;
one of us would've landed on the pole.
But since we were together, we
   fell to the left and the right.
What a twist of fate that was—
   what a blessing in disguise.

A Great Deal

for Jeff Heveron

    I was sorry you couldn't make it to the Open Mic last night, Jeff. I had this poem I wrote about you that I was planning to read as a surprise when you arrived. That isn't totally true. The poem is not written yet — but it's floating in my head.

    I was thinking about a great deal you gave me when you were five years old. Your parents were having a garage sale; and you had a few things for sale too. You offered me a three-foot tall, sturdy wood-and-metal hand truck for one dollar. I didn't think I needed a hand truck; it was rusty and its strap was broken. But you were earnestly smiling, sure of yourself, and I was unable to resist. I paid the dollar, took the truck home.

    The funny thing is — I have used it dozens of times over the years. Yesterday, I used it to haul some yard debris from a torn-down shrub out to the curb. The red army-belt type strap still hangs, half-missing, from the handle, so I attach bungee cords and wrap them around my load. The hand truck is solid as a full-sized one, and I've often thought what a bargain it was — probably the best dollar I have ever spent. Many times, it has saved me from straining my hip and back.

    I tried to call you to remind you to come and bring your poetry, but your voice message says to try again later. Your Facebook page says you don't check in much — I wonder what you're up to now, Mr. Entrepreneur.

    I'm going to start the poem like this:

Thanks for the hand truck, Jeff.
It's been mighty helpful to me in my life.
And it always makes me think of you,
the way you held it out to me, so young
and sure. It was a great deal.

Triggered Memory

Two mornings, Mary, after
you asked me if I could recall
Bobbie Chipperini, I thought that
I saw three little reindeer, the size
   of rabbits, running through tall
grasses on my neighbor's terrace.

As I walked along our backyard alley—
sun in my eyes—I realized the dream—
   of what Bobby had promised:
He said he had access to little
baby reindeer, monkeys and
lambs, elephants, and giraffes.
He said he would bring them
to me one day, so I could play
with them, there on the lawn.
Only three years old at the
   time, I believed every
word with my longing.

What amazes me now,
   is how I hung on—
decade after decade—
to an image from the hope
of a child still inside me—
and that only the mention
of Bobby Chipperini released
   a mirage of miniature
reindeer running past
me in front of my eyes.

Sangha

What holds this
silent community
together—
        all
present
for different
reasons
        still
the practice
is what we
have in common
Being in the
        moment
then letting it go
not-trying
un-tying
loosening knots
trying not to spin it,
trying not to win
        pausing
hands resting
on thighs or laps
Inhaling the now
Exhaling the past
        Holding
the silence
        Inside
letting it
burn to
        ash.

Fall

Now Your Words

Now your words come
tumbling out of the eaves
like leaves from October
maples, one day waving
  goodbye to the sun
shimmering in the sky,
then darkly blanketing
sidewalks and lawns
in crimson and umber,
as if to say — *I told you so.*
Do not take umbrage
with me.   You wanted
the heat of summer to wane;
you moaned and complained,
like you do every year, though
I told you it would not last
any longer than other
years — remember?

The days are numbered,
like your life, whose
reasons and seasons
are kept under wraps
in afterlife scrap books—
This is what made you happy?
This is what made you stop crying?
This is what made you suck in
your breath and know, even
  for a second, that you
      really do get it—
You're waking up now.

A Rolling Bottle Of Wine

for Laura, Bob, Tess

On the night she got pregnant,
Laura was at the Little Theatre
with Bob, pouring wine into
cups in the dark, enjoying
  a romantic comedy,
whose title escapes
her now. She laughed,
  when she told me:
I always bring wine
  to the movies.

That night a slight
shuffle of her feet
back under the seat
caused the bottle to fall
and begin to roll. The floor
declined from back to front;
the bottle kept rolling, and rolling,
between patrons legs all the way to
the front of the quiet theater, until it
hit the stage, finally getting its break.

Laura stopped drinking wine
    for the next nine months.
and Tess was born on time.

Leila In My Arms—

Shevah laid a burping cloth
  on my shoulder and tiny
  little Leila in my arms; she
handed me a 2 oz. baby bottle.
Now and then, Leila sucked the
nipple between jabbering sounds—
Is she humoring me, I wondered?
Is she subtly checking out my
  qualifications, seeing if I
  can work with my hands?
Mindfully working toward
  the perfect bottle angle,
it's hard to believe I was never
a mom. As an older sister to five
of six siblings, an aunt to a dozen
  marvelous beings, all growing
  like Russian olive trees
I try to recall the last
  time I held an infant—
The Galatians implied—
  those who are barren
  will have many children.
Josh and Shevah generously
grant me grandmother status,
as Leila plays the baby for awhile,
with her quick smiles, her esoteric
sounds, her deep ocean eyes and short-
lived subordination. I wonder again
about the dreams I have had since
  her conception was announced.
I'm a girl! I heard her say that
  night in my dream. I gaze
into her deep wise eyes—and
it is mine that spill the tears.

Mystie

You ponder the placement
of a patch of morning sunlight,
then pounce to capture its warmth.
You keep its rays to yourself for awhile.

Then your warm little body
        leaps onto my lap.
And I wish you long life—
        even longer than mine,
though I know that's unlikely.

I let go of these thoughts
        like falling-down sand
through a child's open hands.
        You settle in to purring,
pure and soundly content.

You have pondered all that is:
        There is only one Sun.
It rises up in the morning;
        bows down when it's done.

Painted Lady

Right after she
was paid for, the
red and purple
painted-lady
corner house,
proud porch
stretched across
her front,
suffered from
an arsonist who
left her empty
and charred.

It was months,
at least, before
she ceased to be
the neighborhood *eyesore*—

Finally repainted,
repaired and
re-sold, she
stands abashed
today,
wearing only
charcoal gray.

My Burning Question

I read the news today—
A window washer falls
forty-seven floors
to the ground,
and lives.
A family pet bites
their eight-year-old
child, who then dies.
What keeps us all
from going insane?
The window washer's
doctor marvels at a miracle.
But what about the good
parents of the small child—
  owners of the puppy?
If we all pray, how,
I wonder, do the mother
and father, surviving the loss
of their innocent child
. . . go on living?
And how do those
reveling in God's grace
figure out how to soften
the brutal blows others are
simultaneously suffering?
How do we look one
another in the eye?
This is my burning
question of the day.
  Today
    and every day.

Be True To Your School

This morning
  a radio disc
  jockey played
Be True To Your School
  by the Beach Boys
  and dedicated it
"to all the kids
who are starting
school today,"
      and
"to all the kids
who are starting
school yesterday."

Alone in the shower,
I raise my hand:

Question—
Where did
that deejay
go to school?

Missing Dad

Curtained in the shower,
  I let my tears flow—
down with fresh water
  all that they hold.

Aren't you coming back, Dad?
You've been gone for years—
It never gets any easier—
without you on Earth.

There is a hole in our family;
you kept the peace. You took our coats
in one arm, held out a glass of wine.
You lit up a room with your class.

With the fewest words, you
expressed the most. Between
your wit and tender heartedness,
you could always reach us.

We watched you try to contain
  your laugh—you stretched
  it out and brought it back—
you drew us all in to your joy.

You played such smooth music—
  and you created cartoons—
You radioed in code, Dad—
  messaging, messaging.

Aren't you coming back, Dad?
You've been gone for years.
Curtained in the shower,
I let loose these tears.

Statue Of My Father

If I were an artist, I'd
sculpt a statue, tall as
my Dad, six foot four.
Starting from the floor,
I'd build his body from
the kitchen cupboard—
forty-four Farrell Terrace
where we used to climb up
on a chair to reach the shelf
of favorite cookies, and Ritz
crackers. His legs, I'd make
from adding machine tapes,
swim fins for his feet. His long-
range GE radio, which I now have,
would be his heart. No longer does
it dial up or down, but had, in its time,
such a great sound. His neck would be
made from a Ginger Ale glass, on which
I would wrap a striped red tie, a reminder
of his infinite ties to us, as well as his best
dressed look. I'd make his arms from
camera lenses, and ham radio parts,
his call letters — KJ2P — on his back.
His head would be the framed India ink
contour drawing I did of his smiling
face, taking it all in — finding the humor
in everything. I'd cover his eyes with his
slip-over plastic sunglasses, and place his
Buick Skylark key in his hand, just in case
he wanted to drop down from Heaven some
middle-of-the-night, and take it — for a spin.

Julia's Odyssey

Which hand? you ask,
hiding black lavender
soap behind your back.
Closing my eyes, I inhale,
over and over. You laugh:
You'll smell all the scent out!

I saved it for months, on the sill of
my window, wrapped in crinkly rice
paper. Like the Flower Girl photos—
　in our fall wedding album,
　it's full of your laughter,
your tenderness and youth,
　your splashes in the pool,
your patent leather shoes.

I inhale and remember,
　you cut all your hair,
to give to a stranger,
　a woman with bad news.

Now you're moving to Memphis—
pack your friends in your heart,
leave behind your Brownie dress—
put your cell phone on charge.

Julia-from-Ohio, kiss Virginia
　goodbye—give your friends
and neighbors your big-eyed sigh.
　You are *moving* to Memphis—
　it's not an odyssey of the mind.

Marti's Poem

My words can't hold a tiny
little candle to you. These
   lines are just bare feet
to your hundred pair of shoes.

You appear in a room, flash
   your thousand watt smile—
Without even trying, you
   raise the meaning of style.

Before I get my coat off, you've
   made a dozen new friends.
And each one will be there for you—
   from that moment 'til the end.

You assume success,
and it comes right along—
  like a puppy on a leash—
you've got a new hit song.

You are a whiz on the internet,
at Trader Joe's and Chico's too—
You always find a bargain—
and you are high-tech cool.

You overbook your days, but
  somehow make it through.
You find some time on sale
  and toss it in your stew.

You're my youngest sister,
   I raise my glass to you—
I would've put this in a poem,
but I really thought you knew.

Why Is It

Why is it that I simultaneously
feel both hungry and satisfied?
How is it that I sometimes feel
yawning tired and wide awake?
Why is it that sometimes the
day seems to drag and fly
at the same time?
Why is it that sometimes
I can't think of anything
to write about except for
thousands of things?
Why is it that on a day when
I walked all morning, I feel
like I haven't had any exercise?
Why is it that when I spend
all day at my computer,
I'm physically drained?
How is it that my tender heel
can throb and yet feel normal?
How is it that I can miss someone
and not want to talk to or see them?
How is it that I love my cat so much
it aches, yet I wish she'd leap off my lap?
How is it that meditation is both pure
pleasure and yet, sometimes, torturous?
How is it that my need for connection
with people is always there, and my
need for quiet, alone time is always there too.
Why is it I think so much is not worth repeating—
yet I hate when I forget to recall a stray thought or
line — to write it down and see if it leads me anywhere.

How Was New York?

for Mary

You didn't tell me you were leaving
this time — as if it were nothing, as
if you were slipping into the
bedroom to check on your
child, make sure he was
sleeping, clothes in the
hamper, toys put away.
So, how was New York?
   Did you help move
Eric to some crazy new
digs where his roomies
are cool musicians too?
Has he got his own shelf
   in a functional fridge?
What is the vibe of the
neighborhood? Is there
a hip place to stay nearby?
Did you go out for brunch
at some movie-scene diner
where they will soon know
his name? Is he closer to his
sound work and clubs where
he will sit in and jam? So *this*
was your holiday? Riding back
home in the van — the worries
in your head softening slightly
as you stared out the windows,
trying not to nap, correcting the
papers that were laying in your lap?

White Sky

I have to look twice every time
   the sky is white, like it
is today, rain needling
   into the dry earth below.

Like viewing a late Monet
   (after his eyes were old, weak)
its sky so pale, I clean my
   glasses, and wonder *Is it me?*

Or is God making conference
   calls, teaming up senior staff
in His sky blue meeting rooms
   behind faint gaseous doors?

Lying on the floor, I gaze out
   a window, wishing the wind
would blow those lazy washed-out
   clouds around; break up their bloat.

The soothing blue we take for
   granted is absent, and we're
left, like a forgotten child at
   bedtime, with our hunger.

Then, like steam dissipating
   from a morning bathroom mirror,
some faint baby blue appears—
   as those ghostly clouds recede.

Constant Fire

Between the jazz and blues of daily life,
she finds a soulfulness that sets afire
the unseen fuel lying everywhere
upon the path. She feels a constant fire,
a relentless faith, an assurance that
there is real worth — purpose to her life.

Her tonsils, removed back in grammar
school to improve her hearing left her
speechless, her throat burning and sore.
Now even more isolated than she was
before, she gets behind in school. In some
ways, she feels like she never caught up.

But in slips a gift of vision, between that
year and her teens — an acuity to catch
the drift or the gist of what's going on
by means other than hearing or speech.

Missing half the dialogue, the lyrics of life—
she seeks for clues and finds her cues—
that kiss, or kick — that soulfulness—
that sets afire the unseen fuel along life's
path. And in between the jazz and blues
of daily life — she digs the groove.

I Fall In Love Too Easily

with respect to Keith Jarrett

Now I remember why I stopped playing
my Keith Jarrett — at the Blue Note CDs:
I played them until they wore out.

*I Fall In Love Too Easily/The
Fire Within* now skips hopelessly.
   More than any other, this
piece transports me to a place
of unrelenting longing and loss.
Hearing its tenderness does
   not promise healing.
   It offers a basic comfort—
that we are not alone in a finite
world in the depths of our pain.

The profound exile of notes
and phrasing of this nocturne
   gives us a chance to grasp—
   we truly have only this
   moment.   These spare
keyboard sounds, one drum
   beat propelling the next,
until the phrasing steps up
and we rise to our feet, chest
   lifted, feeling — knowing
   after this melody, life
   will be altered — with deep
gratefulness for he who wrote
   and those who played, from
their gut, this startlingly graceful
adagio, who played it as if the
curtain was truly about to fall.

Ginkgo Tree

for Richard and Lucinda

I wish I'd taken a snapshot
of your wild-with-yellow
Ginkgo tree, before it began
shedding its thorny pods
and fanning leaves.

A tree twice the height
of your home — too
giant to be fake,
yet all its branches
stretch straight out
like a mother's arms—
calling her children back
home.   As you reach the last
few hundred feet before the back
path to Highland Park, it stuns you
with its yellow glory — Yes, yellow—
the opposite of budding, bragging
purple lilacs, for which the park is
known.   Yellow in the Autumn!
Yellow when other trees are red,
brown, orange or evergreen.
Your yellow Ginkgo owns
Gregory Hill Road, until
it gives in to seasonal pressure—
before it paints the sidewalk
with sleeping dreams
of lemonade stands.

Cleaning My Room

How did these items become a part
   of my life's clutter to begin with?
On my desk are two copies of the book,
Yoga for Pregnancy, though I've never
been pregnant. Both books have been
borrowed many times, always returned
with one-line scribbled on a sticky note.
Inside a box of fabric-remnants, snaps,
Velcro, zippers and thread, I find an old
   Yoga Journal, featuring an article, "Be
Happier Than You Ever Thought Possible."
   Have I read it? I cannot recall.
Underneath is a small black and red
journal, one full-moon dated entry
reminding me that, after chanting
in the Kannon Room with my angel-
friend Cynthia, (Dad's photo on the
altar), I returned to the parking lot
to the stunning sight of my car's
front windshield hosting a mass
   gathering of yellowjackets.
   The Buddha of compassion
gave space to my grief, bowed
   kindly to my tears that day.
It was both healing and unbearable.
   That journal, with its one entry,
was buried with all the mending
materials that I own. Yellow-jacket,
as a totem, means *communication*.
   And yellowjacket hosts
   my father's name:
Jack.

Your Untitled Artwork

Memo to you beautiful people — you painters
and other artists, who refuse to name your
work, other than *Untitled*, or *Seated*
  Figure No. 3 — Can We Talk?

When I see one of your wonderful works
left *un-named*, I want to circle my posse
around you, block the studio door. If you
won't do it yourself, I feel *entitled* to try.

Within the frame sits a woman, wearing a
hard-brimmed hat, shading her large dark eyes.
Loosely her hand holds a long blue scarf.
Amber light casts from the window — dawn?
Or dusk? Who knows! Has she just removed the scarf
or she is putting it on, to go. You must know — tell us!

You might have named it *Off the Shoulder,* or *Indecision.*
What about *Indigo Scarf — Long Night?* What day is it?
Has she been forgotten on her birthday? Has she
lost her lover or friend? It is both mournful
and impenetrable. Is she *Reconsidering?*
Has she now realized — *It Is Over?*

Let's get together—
you with your easels and paint;
we with our thesaurus and muse.
This *Untitled* business must stop.
Lay bare your still-wet canvas;
we'll give you a thousand words.

So Far Away

The bloat of the full moon backed
off just a sliver last night. I felt
it finally release us, like retrograde
Mercury's three week snarlup dance.
What pull and power these celestials
have — so much we do not understand.

We think it's just God and us,
oceans, plants, animals, trees
and earth, mountains and sand.
We glance at the clouds as we slip
out the door — but only to check
our need for an umbrella or hat.

Whipping on a scarf, we take
off with a whirl of assumptions
about coming back. Out we go
on our presently good legs, shiny bikes,
or in our swift cars, never knowing
what place these planets and moons
hold in our lives, as they lead and follow
our whole earth around, day after
day, year after year, century after
century of sun, moon, planets,
all in their usual places, never
failing at *their* revolutions
so far anyway.
So far away.

Winter

In the Kitchen

No one ever made sweet promises
   to her in the bedroom of her
   early nineteen hundreds home.
But in the kitchen — with its open shelves,
   laden with spices, cook pans and pots,
   notebooks of hand-written recipes,
      Mason jars full of lentils and rice,
bulgur and beans — in that kitchen —
     three men, over the years,
     whispered *I love you*—
as she diced garlic and onions;
as she sautéed celery and peppers;
as she tore orange sections away from
their thick skins; as she strained cooked
 spaghetti over the old porcelain sink.

She always assumed it was the kitchen
   they loved — with its bare wood floor.
She removed the buckling linoleum,
   tore out a layer of faded tiles underneath—
exposing a solid maple sub-floor. Energized
   by the vibrating power of a rented floor sander,
she removed decades of dirt, hardened adhesive.

Ed, who owned the True Value Hardware Store
talked her out of adding a laminate. *Leave it alone*,
   he said — *even the snow won't hurt that maple*.
She rubbed it with tung oil; left it at that.

She always wondered if the women who lived there
   before her gave the kitchen its allure.

After Valentine's Day

for Emma LeStrange

Having given up
the charade
of freshness,
of forecasting Spring,
long-stemmed
mauve colored
tulips sagged, their
wide heads hung
  over the side of
the proud little vase,
their faces grazing
my cool marble table,
seeking release.

With afternoon light waning fast,
  I dashed for the camera.

Beside the swollen
  blossoms,
  an unopened
heart-shaped tin
  held gold-foil-
covered chocolates.

This gift from tender
teenaged hands
  glistened
with promise.

Landsdale Street

I used to be jealous of Lansdale Street—
whose display seemed better than Benton
   Street — where I lived, just two blocks away.
Lansdale Street had giant trees, providing
   summer with heat-calming shade. And
man, those bragging maples hustled spring,
   rustled the nights of summer along,
   flashed their couture every autumn.

When they shamelessly shed their bright
leaves, the wind blew Autumn to its knees.
   And still I envied Lansdale Street—
   its houses and sidewalks, those trees!

Then there was that rough winter storm—
   the one that froze falling rain.
In a matter of hours every trunk, branch,
and twig was coated with a glistening ice glaze.

Lansdale Street was selected by that storm,
long limbs tore down like war and thunder.
And because of that storm, lovely Lansdale
   Street lost every tree it had known.

I used to be jealous of Lansdale Street.
(It's not something of which I am proud.)
Now I go out of my way to walk down Lansdale Street,
to check on the growth of its new young trees.

My Sister's Closet

for Marti Ponton

Your closet is the size
of my entire backyard.
Do you ever get lost in
there — amidst the earth-
   tone long-sleeved blouse
section? Or the natural fabric
   casual summer slack section?

Ever not find your way back
to the bedroom or the kitchen?
Maybe you're in there right now,
lost, crippled by too many options.
Do you never fear getting strangled
by that gaggle of designer scarves
and belt-ware? Or that you'll trip,
as your satin sling-back slipper
snags on a stray strap
from the wall of open-
toed, low-heeled short-
skirt shoe section? I
peeked in a drawer that
I thought would be your
lingerie dresser, only to
discover, it was your jewelry
box, laden with dazzling gems,
helplessly-captive necklaces,
enviously waiting to be chosen.
The lingerie dresser, of course,
was in an adjacent room, a simple
private room with only a skylight—
soft designer peach walls, ceramic
   sink and washer for delicates,
hand-embroidered silk hamper.

How brilliant to have included
the espresso-maker in there!
You need a cappuccino, while
you wait in the lounge chair,
for the soak cycle to end.
And that antique magazine
rack sure found its home
there, eh? At any rate,
I was just wondering,
Marti, as I descend to
my basement, to toss
in the washer, a load
of all my jeans — if you
ever find, (as I often do),
with that lavish, lofty,
titanic, cavernous closet
of yours — that the one,
single, perfect blouse
that you wanted
so much to wear
today — happens
to be in the wash?

I thought so.

Drano

Most people called him Drano. When we learned his real name was Duane, we started calling him that. He was a Navy SEAL Vietnam War veteran with mental disabilities, who was also a homeless drag queen. He was easily ticked off and went on verbal rants. When we least expected it though, he would smile broadly, laugh and seem genuinely happy. Those moments were fleeting. He borrowed money all month long from various Coconut Grove business owners, and people he befriended who worked in the shops. When he received his disability check, he cashed it and went around paying everyone back.

More than a few times he got beaten up and robbed of the cash before he got this done. So, having nothing left for himself, he started borrowing again. Some mornings, when we arrived at 10:00 o'clock to unlock our record store, *Happy Note*, he was still asleep — blocking the entrance.

Other mornings we found him cooking bacon, eggs, potatoes and toast on a make-shift grill near the loading dock in the back of our store. He often shared this dubious feast with our manager, Tom, who didn't worry that the food might have come from the Winn-Dixie dumpsters. We offered to let Duane sleep in the storage shed behind our store; but he felt safer in more open places where someone might at least see him if he was injured.

Inside the store, he stashed some of his belongings in an empty record bin. He had small stashes in several other stores and he had a grocery cart he pushed around most of the time. When my husband and I didn't have time to go out to lunch or home for dinner, we asked Duane to bring us some take-out food from one of the Coconut Grove restaurants. He took our money and brought back sandwiches in a brown bag, swearing all the while. He prefaced everything with damnation. He was angry, but often in a humorous kind of way and no one took it personally. We paid him for his favors.

My last year in Coconut Grove, Duane gave me a Christmas ornament he made himself — he knit red and white yarn to look like a pair of ice skates, paper clips for blades, laces tied together. I was touched; they were boutique quality. We sold our record store the following year and moved to upstate New York. I heard that Duane eventually died of lung cancer. We all smoked way too much back then.

I've forgotten the names of some of my best customers at the Happy Note and many of our employees. It's been almost thirty years. But every year I hang Duane's knit skates over a Christmas tree branch. And every year I think about him swearing up a storm, pushing his shopping cart around, doing errands for tips, falling asleep on concrete, borrowing and repaying loans, cooking on a sticks-and-stones grill, and knitting Christmas gifts.

Plain View Press Writer's Party

At the party — the party our
   publisher is holding for us,
I forget to bring my three-ring
   binder of new poems,
or, for that matter, even
   a copy of my book.

I spent weeks gathering
the new poems, revising,
reprinting, placing in clear
plastic sleeves. It is not only me—
almost everyone is bookless
when Susan asks us to read.

We Google ourselves, find
our writing here and there—
read poems off a laptop or
a hand-held Blackberry—
(Susan calls them blueberries.)

No one hogs the stage;
      there is no stage.
We are in a circle in Susan's suite,
listening, snacking, sipping wine.

After we read our poems, someone says,
  These are great — someone should
publish *these people!* Everyone glances
at Susan, smiling broadly, nodding,
her long tresses hiding nothing.
  Our grateful laughter *ensues*.

The Man For Whom I Used To Long

So many times he slipped in and out of my life.
For years I would search faces in a crowd,
        any crowd — hoping to find him.
Yet, when he appeared, this time — smiling broadly,
walking toward me in the lobby of the Sheraton Hotel,
        I did not even see him — until
he was close enough to kiss me on the lips.
I was with my husband, who was amused but unfazed,

At first, I wished I'd worn my Italian red leather jacket,
        instead of my lavender fleece Patagonia.
I wished I'd tied my silk scarf in a loose Milan-style knot.
        I wished I'd had my camera out, taken a shot.
I wished I'd written something obscure inside the copy
        of my book he bought — inside the space where
        April's dreamlike figures float above clouds.
Something like: *Thanks for the blackberry tea.*

None of this matters at all.
        With a shrug, I released him
        to the revolving doors—
                to the street.
At last, I am with a man he can't unhinge,
        in a relationship he cannot topple.
And he saw it;
        he saw it instantly.

Odessa

Odessa worked on
my aching feet as if she
were auditioning for
the gig, but I was only
a Montreal tourist she
may never see again.

She used the kind of pressure
   that stuns. Her hands
   were so strong, I said—
If you ever need to get free
   from an unwanted grip,
   I bet you could flip
a man on his back.

She smiled, with a peace-
   fulness that let me
   drop off to sleep,
drop my need to talk,
   drop my fear of pain.

What could I exchange
   for this labor of hers?
I would drive all day
   for her brand of care.

But my hour with her
   was all about me;
I left — knowing not
   what she needs.

Monterey

That was back in Monterey;
　I thought that we would be fine.
We were married, we had our day.

I thought we'd never be dismayed;
　we knew so little at the time.
That was back in Monterey.

You could have had the last say—
　I was clearly out of my mind!
I thought that we would be fine.

When it was cold, I began to pray,
　took everything as a bad sign—
that was back in Monterey.

We didn't know how to meet halfway
　or, how on earth — to be kind.
I thought that we would be fine.

I realized that I could not stay
with you; we were both purblind!
　That was back in Monterey—
we were married; we had our day.

Isobel Illusion

for Stephanie and Michael

Squinting up from
under my toweled
loosely- piled,
heap of hair,
I think
I see
a couple
embracing in
your doorway.

And it is not
an ordinary
embrace—
It is a post-
World War II front
page photo embrace.

But as I reach up to
rearrange my head-wrap
for a better view, I realize
it is only an optical illusion—
the happenstance way the jackets
and hats hang on your coat rack.

But surely, somewhere, at this very
moment, two people are standing
in a doorway, just as I see them,
embracing like the war is over.

Coffee Shop Scene

Outside the glass wall,
   snow falls as salt—
   from a sky shaker.
Inside, satirical artwork
   plasters the facing
   brick wall. It's late
morning; musicians
   drag in. Baristas
have stopped hissing
   and fussing. Empty
mugs sit, foam drying,
   on wobbly tables,
creased muffin wrappers
   hint at cranberry.
Laptops glow as
patrons, sitting alone,
post notes on Facebook.

The morning paper, tossed
   from sticky hands to
   crumb-skewed chairs
screams a local headline—
   now old news to all.
Couch slipcovers crawl
   toward the floor. The
     lighting is poor.
Why do we stay?
Clapton is wailing: *Well*
if I've done somebody wrong,
Lord, have mercy if you please.

Boarding the Plane

Boarding the plane,
buckling my seatbelt,
mindlessly sliding a carry-on
   bag beneath the seat ahead—
over the speaker, the stewardess
says: *In the event of a water landing—*
(It's all so routine, even for me.)

But this flight follows
two recent crashes,
both in my home state
both on my mind.
One pilot, a hero for saving
the lives of everyone aboard,
the other pilot gone, along
with all of his passengers,
and a man casually
watching TV in his
family room, struck dead;
his family torn asunder,
homeless.

The first set of passengers
had time to cry out or pray—
a moment to dial a number—
to say goodbye, but lived—
gliding into the Hudson River—
a miraculous water landing.

The second flight is steeped
 in icy mystery. No stressful
voiced last words; still—
everyone is gone.

There was no rhyme or reason, no
seasoned clarity, no flying slumber.
no shifting of odds—
    there was
no strength in numbers.

One half hour from our landing,
the stewardess offers up a tray—
small glasses of chardonnay
and I wonder what we
might be celebrating.

From my window, all I can see
is a layer of billowy clouds—
the sky like a frozen
snow-covered pond.

And I have a moment
to cover my eyes.

January-March

Cold as it's been I hate to see
      winter wane
since once that starts—
      we're into spring
and winter is on its way again.

All the imagined
      Silence—
bunkering down
with music and books
in front of a fireplace
warming our feet—
those days never last
long enough for me.
Purging and gathering,
mending, and sewing,
compiling music tapes,
creating birthday cards
and lyrical lines — where
are those slow motion days?

As I find time for Photoshop
   and Facebook, I face the fact of my
youth well-spent and life, generously,
   letting me in on another era.

Empty Oil Tank

We awoke to a
freezing
cold house
one Saturday
morning in March,
having run flat out
of heating oil. Thank
God for a sun-basked
couch, and one cool cat,
who rose to the occasion
of our complete panic.
She leapt to our laps,
purred steadily 'til
our oil supplier
replied to our
pleading call.
This year, he
said, the cost
of oil will increase
by seventy percent.
I wonder how many
cats we could keep and feed for that.

I Feel You Kicking

for Liz and Lexie

It takes a good twenty five minutes to drive
   from Brighton to the Seneca Park Zoo.
The ride seemed longer for Lexie,
strapped in her car seat in back,
   than it was for her mother, Liz
   driving up front in the van.

Lexie passed the time kicking
the seat back in front of her feet.
Liz only laughed and called out—
   I feel you kicking, Lexie!

Those words reverberated with
   irony—punctuating her kicks.
Lexie was adopted as a baby;
(the womb she kicked was not Liz's).

Lexie enthusiastically entertains us,
singing songs and reciting rhymes.
   She loves to dance on her toes;
   her skirt spins out to all sides.
It's easy to forget she's so young—
as she mugs, mimics and mimes.

She came into this family for a reason—
   many people who love her are here.
If she's noticed her mocha skin
does not quite match her folks,
   I am *relatively* certain
   she does not really care.

Don't Say It (Insomniac)

You've said it so many times—
   you've said:
I'll end up an insomniac.
   and yet, you sip
   caffeinated chai
into the evening,
   you move a TV
   into your bedroom,
you nap after work,
   make dinner late,
bring books to bed—
all the things against
   which they warned
at the sleep clinic.

Why don't you respect
   the prospect
and habit of sleep,
   sound and blessed—
like the deep mystery
   of the ocean,
like the motion
   of the planets,
like the shifting
   of the seasons
when you're falling
     in love—
like the ritual rising
   and setting
of the sun?

Hoselton Toyota Waiting Room

A car dealership is a hard place to relax
It's a place of separation and fear.
Though the men mostly pace,
women seem to bring things
to occupy their time: knitting,
sewing, reading, folders full of
coupons. The sight of hundreds of
cars in the massive lot doesn't entice
me to go for a walk. And knowing the longer
I wait, the higher the cost could be, keeps me
on the edge of my seat. Three annoying TVs
provide further unwanted distraction. I think:

*There should be a gym—with exercise bikes
or elliptical trainers. How 'bout a nail salon,
or at least a real coffee shop, not just a stale pot.
A library would be nice — with something more
meaty than car magazines. Why doesn't some
college or high school art class loan some of their
projects? These posters of cars do not soothe
my eyes. Oh, where is my car? My partner in travel?*
There is shopping nearby — errands stack up in my mind,
   but the thing I'm without, is the thing that I need—
my car! I am sitting here jiggling my legs, wasting
my time, while my car is in the spa for a day.

At last, my paperwork and keys are left
at the desk. My name is called, with the
ambiguous statement: *You're all set.*

Not Cleaning My Room

A long skirt I made to wear to a wedding
   eight years ago sits on my desk,
ready to morph into a guest room
   curtain. I open and refold the fabric;
That marriage has ended.

Fifty feet of used and re-used speaker-wire,
   wound neatly, and tucked away, reminds
   me of simpler stereos, of splicing wires
in my bamboo-walled studio in Coconut Grove.

Why do I keep all these non-working pens?
   I wore them out writing in long-hand
to family and friends, paying my
   bills and respects, sharing my secrets
with one spiral-bound notebook after another.

Baskets of business cards, boxes of buttons
from a local out-of-business factory,
once used as bingo markers at the
shelter for battered women, a set of
marking pens, yards of ribbon and trim,
movie tickets stubs, and live music programs—
shall I file them in chronological order for
when I am older, can't remember my life?

I look at the skirt again; pick up
the phone and call the friend.

That Song

Wrong as the porridge, the chair,
and the bed Goldilocks first tried,
   that song was too big, too hot,
too hard for her voice—like a
hand-me-down dress she would
   never have chosen herself.

The second song was wrong
   like the mama bear's
porridge, chair, and bed—
   too big, too cold, too soft.
It was a gray song and gray
is for wildlife, she said. (She
is wildly addicted to fuchsia
   and cerulean blue.)

The third song was just right
like a custom made dress she
could slip right over her head.
   She heads to rehearsal with
verve, embarks on a path she knows,
   to sing a song from the soul of
   the writer, that speaks to the
singer, who soothes the listener.

That is the song that we need, the one
   that when sung helps us breathe.

AWP — NYC 2008

We are writers with name tags,
   and AWP tote bags, surrounded
by seven thousand writers with
   name tags and identical tote
bags in hand holding schedules
   of novel events, readings,
various books and pens,
our Moleskine journals.

Only a few blocks away
   striking T.V. writers
pace, carrying signs.
I ask a striker if he
knows about the
writer's event
up the street.
No, he says,
shaking his head,
handing me a flyer.

They used to make
television entertaining.
Now, it's been so long
without new episodes—
we are all getting out more,
   and out of the habit
of watching T.V.

A Former Beau

She used to keep
one wool
sweater
that held
his scent
for when
he went
away—

until he
betrayed her,
lied about
another—

woman,
how quickly
that dark
blue sweater
got washed
and shrunk
then tossed
away.

The Trouble With Winter

It is not the snow or the cold,
   not even the wind or the ice.

Nor is it the darkness of daybreak
   or indigo evenings.
It isn't the smell of exhaust
or that it blackens the snow,
   like an insult.

It is not the lost glove,
   or the cold wet sock,
when your foot lands too deep
   in a hollowing snow bank.
It isn't chapped lips, cracked fingers
   or skin that begs to be scratched.

It is not losing your keys in a darkened
   white void. It's not even the fear
of slipping on ice, breaking your
   leg or wrecking your car.

It isn't the stillness, or having
to   slow   down   your   life.

The trouble with winter is knowing
the homeless roam freezing at night
   as you pull up your blankets
   and whisper your prayers.

Spring

New Life Gossip

for Richard and Grace

Right — Poetry Is Not Memoir—
voice of the poem, yada, yada.
Are you kidding me? Did you
see him with her? Have
you *read* his new book?
Those love poems rise up
like hot air balloons at the
Bristol Balloon Festival—
purple, yellow, red, green,
and oh, my gondola—
when his shoulders
press into hers, tweed
jackets or not — you
know what I'm saying?
They were sizzling like
bacon on a griddle at
an Eddie Rocket Diner.
They had their lesson plans,
books, their serene teacher
faces — all-is-copasetic looks.
But when she lifted her
eyes to glance at him,
he felt it right through
the back of his head.
I'll tell you this, girlphone—
that new book of his? He
is just getting warmed up.

Billy and Me

What are the chances, Billy?—
Your name and mine in the same
front page article of *the Democrat
and Chronicle:* mine — for attending
the Jazz Festival, yours—for being
the poet whose book I brought along.

A reporter named Karen, usually
a restaurant reviewer, singled me
out from throngs arriving at the
Rochester Jazz Festival, to ask,
what I had stashed in my tote bag.
Auspiciously, I pulled out your book,
Billy Collins, *The Trouble With Poetry*.
She smiled, *What else did you bring?*
probably hoping for avocado sushi,
lime-drenched mango slices or kiwi.
I removed some tissue, an Acme
pen, a blank Moleskine journal,
a light rain jacket, and mauve
sun glasses by Ralph Lauren.

The one item I did not reveal—
(and I will share this with you,
Billy) — was a fine glass of wine,
concealed in a green tea bottle.
Have you noticed how similar
in color Australian Chardonnay
can be to Arizona Green Tea?
Here's to you, Billy Collins,
for sharing the front page—
with me. Here's to you,
and to Jazz, and to tea.

The Trouble With Reading Your Poems

It's not that I don't trust you, but when I read your poems,
    I wonder if that vase of fresh cut roses you describe
could be fake — could be, that is, an imaginary vase of roses,
    rather than one you actually see on your table.

Is there really a gardenia-scented candle burning in a
darkening kitchen, as the sun sets over the pines outside?
Or are you sitting on the couch, curtains drawn, an old
    lamp you have had forever burning instead?

I know that jar of jam you describe — (as you spread some
on a biscuit) — as *home-made* by your lover — (who tied
the lid with raffia) — might have come from a local grocery
store, made in large vats in a factory, sold everywhere.

You should see outside *my* window, Billy — the terraced
back yard — my neighbor, Nick, with his long-handled
   hose is kindly watering my young Arborvitae
shrubs and black-eyed Susans, ready to pop.

If I wrote a poem, I'd show you my soft new hammock,
    so white and inviting beneath the walnut tree, my glass-
topped umbrella table holding a tray of blackberry tea.
My favorite yellow finch would stop by
    in his little black vest.

Seriously, I wouldn't make this up — I wouldn't even
    know how. I'd take a photo on my cell
phone for proof and send it to you, but
    I don't know how to do that either.
You'll have to trust me.

Memorial Day Rain Rant

The day dawns easy, overcast,
neither hot nor cold, barely
a breeze — flawlessly.
Humidity sneaks
in, like a nest of
snakes. Again
this year, clouds
appear, about to
burst, but they don't
or won't — You want
to shake your fist at
the sky, and shout:
Just RAIN already—
  get it over with!
One lousy day off
for folks from May
'til the Fourth of July!
Chance of showers—
Thunderstorms likely—
Should we call-off
the picnic or not?
Just RAIN already!
RAIN for the cat, who
hides in the basement at
the first shift in barometric
pressure, stays 'til it's over.
RAIN to motivate basil
and tomatoes, planted
today in pots of clay
on the porch. RAIN
the dust off the cars;
we cannot afford to
wash them anymore.

RAIN 'til the trees shake
loose last year's birds' nests.
RAIN 'til the playground
turns to a mosh pit, as
mothers call their kids home.
RAIN to ruin Memorial Day
weekend, like you always do!
RAIN to knock down the tents
and lean-tos people are using
for shelters in broken parts
of the world. RAIN to wreak
havoc on the few remaining
items they might still own.

RAIN 'til the ominous sky is so
black, no one can tell if it's night
or the end of the world. RAIN 'til
the worms crawl out of the ground,
groveling for mercy. RAIN 'til Noah
returns: Noah, who was building his
ark, as everyone laughed — Noah who
gathered pairs of geese, horses, mice,
rabbits, monkeys, elephants and gnats,
as they boarded his floating wood raft.
RAIN 'til the ocean's salt is diluted,
   and only our tears can keep it
in balance. RAIN 'til the darkened
wet street obliterates all shadows.
RAIN 'til a desert meets with a forest
and exchanges ideas. RAIN 'til the
names of the soldiers on all of the
tombstones in all the grave yards
are completely washed clean.

Barely Spring

Don't hesitate to stop—
take a seat on a bench
in a quiet park. Inhale
the tittering laughter
of the youngest toddlers.
Welcome the breeze,
and the way your hair
tickles your cheeks.

Leave your camera behind—
　only take snapshots
in your mind this time.
It's barely spring—no buds
or blossoms abound yet.
School busses still halt,
　crank out their stop
signs and drop children
　off — late in the day.

Last year's decaying leaves
　and broken twigs still
lay on the not yet-green
　grass, useless debris.
There's even a small
mound of snow on the
shady side of the street.
We can't count on anything yet.
We're all in transition here—
the birth of another year.

Not Every Woman Swooned

for Amy and Scott LeStrange

Not every woman swooned;
not every man let out a sigh,
as you strolled down the hill
playing your horn amidst the crowd.

One couple,
        conversing with each other,
barely noticed
        as you passed by.

Earlier they watched their daughter
end her high school years on stage.
As you played those haunting melodies,
their bittersweet day was assuaged.

You extended those soothing notes—
        overtook the Syracuse sky.
The audience rose to their feet—
the couple felt the passage of time.

These events occurred the same day;
        they are forever entwined.
Arm in arm, they went home together,
Facing the future, they let out a sigh.

Breaking Twenties

I break a twenty
to order an espresso
stuff the change
into my winter
jacket. It's sunny,
March twentieth,
first day of Spring—
I think: *Maybe I
won't need this fleece
again for awhile.*
I imagine I'll find
the dollar bills
in my pocket like
a gift next Fall.
Except this is
  Rochester,
New York and
I know better.
Snow is expected
tonight, tomorrow,
Wednesday, Thursday,
Friday. The good thing
is that the forecast
does not go past
then. It should
stay in the low
thirties. It
looks like it
will not break
into the twenties.

National Women's Hall Of Fame

Seneca Falls, New York

We walk towards the
outside wall, where *The
Declaration of Sentiments*
is engraved in stone, the
sound of water running
   over the words slows
our pace as we pause to read,
and press our hands to the words:

*We hold these truths to be self-evident,
that all Men and Women are created equal.*

Inside, we are stunningly
greeted by life-size bronze
statues of women, still
not famous enough for
writing and signing the
declaration in 1848.
It took seventy-two
more years before
women would obtain
the right to vote for a
president in their home country.

Tourists, women who don't
even know one another,
look straight into
each other's welled-up eyes,
and help us all swallow the
gagging lumps in our throats.

Peace Crane

for the Paul Rooney family

There is a peace crane in his Bonsai tree—
   the tiniest one I have ever seen.

Like the flickering
   light of Tinkerbell,
Sonya's folded paper cranes
help to make his patients well.

Her gentle Blue Jay sits
   near a window, still—
faithfully protecting
her father's unique skill.

Inside the door, in bright
   poster-paint pride
is Sylvia's disarming
red, white and blue flag.

Renata's nature photos
   and quilted tapestries,
calm our eyes as he slips
   those needles in with ease.

We arrive for acupuncture
   hoping our pain will lift.
We leave enriched in all
   the Rooney family gifts.

There's a peace crane in that Bonsai tree—
   the tiniest one I have ever seen.

Father Gregg

Father, may I have a moment of your time?
  How often have you heard those words?
You have been at it for over twenty-five years.
How many unavowed Confessions you have you heard?

How many First Communions and Confirmations have you
  hosted? How many times have you whispered Amen?
You have guided so many sweet children
  as they morphed into young women and men.

How many foreheads have you splashed with
  Holy Water — or anointed with blessed oil?
How many Masses have you celebrated?
  You've seen so many facets of this world.

How many pre-marital consultations?
  How many Stations of the Cross?
So many smiles and hearty handshakes—
  as you stand representing their God.

At how many funerals have you spoken, as
  your community — and you — lost loved kin?
How many times have you silently thanked God
  for the solace that came straight from Him?

For sure, more than once, you recalled—
  that when Lazarus died, Jesus wept.
It is obvious to folks, Father Gregg, that
  the vows you have made, you have kept.

He chose you to serve, Father Gregg.
  He called you; and you heard that call.
I just wanted a moment of your time, Father
  to say thank you, thank you — that's all.

After Block Island Poetry Project

We board the ferryboat, trust
our bags to the luggage rack
and stack our handouts and books
in our carry-on totes for the crossing.

The community we became
   for a weekend of writing
floats off like lost feathers
to the four winds. But threads
   of connection crisscross
our future hearts, as we hold
inside what no one can take
from our banks of memory.

Like the Block Island "Easter seals"
   who stay, late in the season,
on warm rocks, I am still there,
   in a parlor armchair, looking
from face to precious face — feeling
your braveness, the slight rise in
   your voice, as you share some
new stretch of words, a poem
   whose ink is still drying
on the paper in your trembling hand—
your unique take on the world,
your sob of a prayer, your secret-
revealed, or long-silent scream.

That gathering of subconscious
thoughts you excavated to share
is the hand that grabbs my arm,
and already is pulling me back.

New Neighbor In the City

for Lisa Seischab

Your blinds are drawn — they finally came!
   I live next door — 20 feet away.
Our shrub is trimmed — this side anyway—
   my welcome to you on a sunny day.

An odd, but common arrangement—
       at home, in our many rooms—
proximity with privacy;
      we all live quite alone.

The leaves hang up tight in the trees,
       holding back their autumn splash.
You arrived just in time for our block party;
       we welcomed you at last.

But we have yet to see your colors—
       will you be removing your mask?
Or will you keep your blinds drawn—
       sticking to private tasks?

This is life in the city, as I see it,
       options, many as the stars—
neighbors, a dog's-walk away — or
       anonymously passing in cars.

I see you've got a new mailbox!
       That old name has been set free.
We heard you play the bassoon—
       did I tell you my cat loves reeds?

Your blinds are drawn—
       they look just great!
I live next door — twenty feet away.

Early Spring

Purple crocuses blossom
in the garden edge spaces
where snow has finally melted.
The multi-branched shadow
of a still-bare tree creeps
across the sun-washed lawn—

A retired man, riding his bike
up a steep driveway discards
his helmet and backpack
on the ground,
like a child—
leaves it for later.

Yard debris appears,
bagged on curbs
like faith offerings
for the coming of Spring.
And hawk soars above,
sure of the big picture.

Highland Park In May

You meant to draw
one of your favorite
Austrian pine trees,
yet somehow a simple
shrub took shape on your
sketch pad — the new growth
of Spring, the stun of fairest greens—
When did they open? — Yesterday
those leaves were barely buds!
      In the same moment,
   the first blossoming lilac
catches your eye — its lavender
scent so sweet, you almost
cry — as you drink up the
      rainbow of
      grape/
      violet/
      purple/
      lavender/
      lilacs.
The first lilac each May
brings dew to your eyes—
for a long-held promise
made good once again
after a cold hard winter.

In Memory Of Doug Fetter

Six bags of mulch lay, unopened,
beside the red and yellow day lilies
on Doug's back lawn next door.
He won't be coming back.

I water the pink, purple, and peach
colored geraniums in a flower box above
   the stone work of his empty house.
I don't think I ever told him how
I loved those colors together.

Recently his emphysema kept him
from doing the gardening he enjoyed.
He told me he smoked for fifty years.
Should've known better, he'd say.
One day he just ran out of breath.

He used to tease me about the weeds
I pulled, the Austrian pine cones
I picked up. *Bet you'd like a dime
for every one of those,* he'd say.
I'd be a millionaire, I would say.

A red tail hawk landed on our
front walk one Sunday morning.
I called over the split-rail—
Hey, Doug — did you see The Hawk?
Most every day, he replied.

He used to sit in his lawn chair,
just out of sight in the open garage—
I should've realized he was a bird watcher—
   back yard full of all kinds of feeders.
Those birds lost a great friend.

I'm so sorry, Nancy, the mail lady,
said when I told her. *He was such
a wise-guy — always gave me
 a hard time*, she smiled.

I stood, holding the garden hose;
 she held the delivery pouch.
*I guess I'll just keep leaving
 the mail*, she said, *until
someone tells me to stop.*

Confiserie Délices

for Sarah Heveron-Smith

Returning to the U.S. from France, encumbered
   with art supplies, new Parisian clothes,
books and souvenirs, you remembered us—
   You brought us dark chocolate pralines.
We savored each one, (and in true Heveron
   fashion, one petite piece still remains).

We thought of you too, exploring old Europe,
learning the fine points of French, their customs,
and rituals. We envisioned you laughing
in Paris, like Audrey Hepburn in *Sabrina*.
One day you will tell your stories — (*l'intrigue!*),
show your sketches, — (*les croquis!*), write
les mémories merveilleux of that notable
year. We would love to know which
moment stands out in your mind,
like a framed old photograph,
which speaks to your soul.

We only know you accomplished
something huge, and amazing.
And we know you held our love
in your pocket, like a lucky
worn coin. And when you
returned, with a slightly
   new smile on your face,
you gave us sweet chocolate.

If This Were the Last Day

If this were the last day
  that you would walk,
what revered place might
  you hike — to reach?

If this were the last day
  that you could hear,
what sounds would soothe
  you through — deaf years?

If this were the last day
  that you had sight,
what precious scene
would you hope — to see?

If this were the last day
  that you had a voice,
what would the lines be
  that you — would speak?

If this were the last day
that you could feel love,
  whom would you
hold — in your arms?

If this were the last day
you were able to think,
  would you dare
to open — your mind?

If today, you had only one wish,
would it be for whole-world peace?
If this were your last day on earth,
what unique gift — would you leave?

About the Author

Elaine Heveron grew up in Rochester, NY, graduated from Villa Maria College in Buffalo and spent 10 years in Coconut Grove, Florida. Her previous book of poetry, *Email To Cleveland* was published by Plain View Press in 2007. She now resides with her poet/attorney husband, Louis Faber and their loving cat, Mystie.

Elaine and Lou enjoy attending writing workshops together at Omega Institute, The Taos Writing Salon, and for the last three years at the Block Island, R.I. Poetry Project. Elaine's poetry is strongly influenced by her love of music, her fascination with people, and the underlying joy she finds in the events of everyday life.

Alphabetical Index Of Poems

A Former Beau	80
After Block Island Poetry Project	96
After Valentine's Day	58
A Great Deal	29
A Little Blessing	28
All You Have Is the Present	11
A Rolling Bottle Of Wine	36
A Rolling Jar Of Honey	18
Aural Love	13
AWP — NYC 2008	79
Barely Spring	90
Be True To Your School	41
Billy and Me	86
Boarding the Plane	70
Breaking Twenties	92
Brick Streets In the South Wedge	16
Cleaning My Room	52
Coffee Shop Scene	69
Confiserie Délices	102
Constant Fire	49
Don't Say It (Insomniac)	75
Drano	62
Early Spring	98
Empty Oil Tank	73
Father Gregg	95
Ginkgo Tree	51
Highland Park In May	99
Hoselton Toyota Waiting Room	76
How Was New York?	47
I Fall In Love Too Easily	50
I Feel You Kicking	74
If This Were the Last Day	103
In Memory Of Doug Fetter	100
In the Kitchen	57

I Set Down	27
Isobel Illusion	68
It Hurts My Eyes To See	14
January-March	72
Julia's Odyssey	44
Landsdale Street	59
Leila In My Arms—	37
Letter to My Soul	20
Lost and Found	23
Lost Journal	22
Marti's Poem	45
Memorial Day Rain Rant	88
Missing Dad	42
Monterey	67
Moutin Reunion	12
My Burning Question	40
My Sister's Closet	60
Mystie	38
National Women's Hall Of Fame	93
New Life Gossip	85
New Neighbor In the City	97
Not Cleaning My Room	77
Not Every Woman Swooned	91
Now Your Words	35
Odessa	66
Ontario Beach Park	21
Painted Lady	39
Peace Crane	94
Plain View Press Writer's Party	64
Sangha	31
Sewing Together, Worlds Apart	24
Shot	25
So Far Away	54
Statue Of My Father	43

Sunflower Dreams   15
Taking My Back Yard Back   26
That Song   78
The Man For Whom I Used To Long   65
The Trouble With Reading Your Poems   87
The Trouble With Winter   81
Triggered Memory   30
Weeds and Words   17
White Sky   48
Why Is It   46
Your Untitled Artwork   53

www.ingramcontent.com/pod-product-compliance
Lightning Source LLC
Chambersburg PA
CBHW052103070526
44584CB00017B/2318